KATHERINE THOMSON is a multi-award winning playwright and screenwriter. Her television credits include *Mr & Mrs Murder, Australia on Trial, Darwin's Brave New World, Rogue Nation, Killing Time, East West 101, Satisfaction, BlackJack, Wildside, Grass Roots, Halifax f.p.* and was the co-writer of the Australian and Canadian co-production *Answered by Fire* which received the Gold AWGIE in 2006. Katherine wrote the documentary *Unfolding Florence—the Many Lives of Florence Broadhurst* which was directed by Gillian Armstrong. It screened at Sundance Film Festival and won the AWGIE Award for Best Documentary and Best Television Script at the Queensland Premier's Literary Awards in 2006.

Katherine's numerous and critically acclaimed theatre credits include *King Tide, Harbour, Diving for Pearls, Barmaids, Fragments of Hong Kong, Navigating, Kayak, Mavis Goes to Timor, Wonderlands* and *Darlinghurst Nights*. In 2006, Katherine was awarded the Australian National Playwrights Centre Award for her substantial contribution to the Australian theatre industry. In 2010 Katherine's play *King Tide* was adapted for ABC Radio Airplay. It won an AWGIE for Best Radio Adaptation. She is currently in development on numerous film and television projects including a feature documentary with director Gillian Armstrong about the acclaimed costume designer Orry Kelly, which is due for release in 2014.

ANGELA CHAPLIN has been involved in professional theatre for over two decades and has directed a number of national and international productions. Angela has been Artistic Director of Arena Theatre Company, Magpie Theatre and deckchair theatre in Fremantle, Western Australia. For deckchair theatre Angela commissioned work and directed plays including *Emma, Barmaids, Factory Girl, Too Far to Walk, Ningali* (which won an Edinburgh Fringe Festival First Award for Best New Production 1995 and a Green Room Award for Best Solo Performer), *Edge, Voices, Waterfront Women, Kate 'N' Shiner, Jimmy & Pat Meet the Queen, This Hospital is My Country, Diving for Pearls, La Heroina Del Dolor, Red Alert, King for This Place*, *Salt*, *Luna*, *Hysteria* and *Romeo & Juliet*. Other directing credits include: *Summer of the Aliens* (Sydney Theatre Company); *Our Path* (Theatre North/Ten Days on the Island Festival); *Matricide – The Musical* (Chanber Made Opera); and *Black Mary* (Combany B, Festival of the Dreaming). In 2002 Angela spent six weeks as director-in-residence at Curtin University.

KAVISHA MAZZELLA an ARIA award winning singer songwriter based in Melbourne, Australia. She has worked on many deckchair shows, notably *Fleets of Fortune*, *Ballad of Lois Ryan*, *John Boyle O'Reilly*, *Emma*, *Waterfront Women* and *Luna*. She has also played at the European Broadcasting Union Music Festival in Miskolc, Hungary, the Australia Festival in Dublin, Ireland and performed in *Women in Voice 10*, Brisbane. She has directed choirs such as the Italian women's choir *La Voce Della Luna* in Melbourne and has won a number of awards, including the 1997 Green Room Award for Musical Direction of *Emma*, an ARIA for her CD *Fisherman's Daughter* (ABC/EMI) in 1998 and Best Female Artist at the Global Music Awards in Thredbo in 2000. Her music can be found at www. kavisha.com.

Mavis Goes to Timor

**KATHERINE THOMSON, ANGELA CHAPLIN &
KAVISHA MAZZELLA**

A work of fiction, based on stories told by
Mavis Taylor, Elwyn Taylor and the women
of East Timor

CURRENCY PRESS
SYDNEY

CURRENCY PLAYS

First published in 2003
by Currency Press Pty Ltd
PO Box 2287, Strawberry Hills, NSW, 2012, Australia
enquiries@currency.com.au
www.currency.com.au

in association with Playbox Theatre, Melbourne

Reprinted 2013.

NATIONAL LIBRARY OF AUSTRALIA CIP DATA

    Thomson, Katherine, 1955–
    Mavis goes to Timor.
        ISBN 9780868197029.
        1. Women—Employment—East Timor—Drama.
        I. Mazzella, Kavisha. II. Chaplin, Angela.
        III. Playbox Theatre (Melbourne, Vic.). IV. Title.
        (Series: Current theatre series).
    A822.3

Typeset by Erin Dewar for Currency Press.
Cover photograph by Jon Green.
Cover design by Katy Wall for Currency Press.
Front cover shows Anne Phelan.

Currency Press acknowledges the Traditional Owners of the Country on which we live and work. We pay our respects to all Aboriginal and Torres Strait Islander Elders, past and present.

Contents

Dedicated to Mavis and Elwyn Taylor and the generous people of East Timor who assisted with this project.

Mavis Goes to Timor was first produced by deckchair theatre for the Perth International Arts Festival on 7 February 2002 with the following cast:

MAVIS	Anne Phelan
ELWYN	Kerry-Ella McAullay
MARIANA	Cidalia Pires
MUSICIANS	Kavisha Mazzella
	Marco Quiroz
	The 'Mavis Goes to Timor' Choir

Director, Angela Chaplin
Set Designer, Michael Betts
Video, Nancy Jones
Lighting Designer, Mark Howett
Costume Design, Mand Markey
Choir Director, Jenny Simpson
Choir Leader, Maria Madeira
Original music and lyrics, Kavisha Mazzella
Additional traditional music from East Timor and a song by Anito Matos

CHARACTERS

MAVIS, an 86-year-old woman from Yarrawonga
ELWYN, her daughter, late 40s or early 50s
MARIANA, a Timorese woman in her 20s
MUSICIANS and CHOIR

SETTING

Mavis Goes to Timor was performed outdoors under the trees and stars. The performance space was flexible, and framed by a series of actual shipping containers which provided various performance levels. These could be opened to reveal rooms such as Mavis's bedroom in Dili or her shop in Yarrawonga, as well as being the container which was packed to go to Dili. On one side of the space was Mavis's living room, on the other a sandy area for the choir and musicians. The roofs of the containers were used for some of the Dili scenes.

Stage directions in this playtext are based on the original production.

ACKNOWLEDGEMENTS

The writers wish to acknowledge inspiration from 'Buibere – Voice of East Timorese Women' compiled by Sally-Anne Watson and the women of the Buibere Books Cooperative, Dili.

INSTRUMENTAL: 'Morning In Dili'

As the audience enters the space, the CHOIR *sings 'Ina Lou'.*

*SONG: 'Ina Lou' (traditional) *

CHOIR:

> *Ita Ema Sei Moris*
> *Halo Rai Nian Naran Ina Lou*
> *Ai Lai Lai Lai Ina Lou*
> *Ai Ita Ema Sei moris*
> *Halo Rai nia Naran Betena.*

> *Mate Ona Rai Taka Tilun*
> *Labe Rona Ina Lou*
> *Ai Lai Lai Lai Ina Lou*
> *Ai Mate Ona Rai Taka Tilun*
> *Labe Rona Betena.*

> CHORUS
> *Lai Lai Ai Lai Lai Lou*
> *Ina Lou Ina Lou*
> *Lolei Kole Lalet Ona Betena*
> *Ai Lai Lai Lai Ina Lou*
> *Ai Kole Lalet Ona Betena.*

> *Lolo Liman La To*
> *Mata Ben Sulin Ina Lou*
> *Ai Lai Lai Lai Ina Lou*
> *Ai Lolo Liman La To*
> *Mata Ben Sulin Betena.*

> CHORUS
> *Lai Lai Ai Lai Lai Lou*
> *Ina Lou Ina Lou*
> *Lolei Kole Lalet Ona Betena*
> *Ai Lai Lai Lai Ina Lou*
> *Ai Kole Lalet Ona Betena* x 3

---

* See Appendix on page 44 for translation of lyrics.

SONG: 'Sleep Sleep' **

> Sleep sleep,
> Darling, sleep sleep,
> Sleep sleep,
> Darling, sleep sleep,
> Close your eyes, close your eyes
> To all the trouble that terrifies.
>
> As long as it doesn't happen to you,
> Who cares for the suffering?
> Anyway, what can you do?
> All we can say
> Is 'We pity those poor',
> All we can say
> Is 'We pity those poor'.
>
> If we speak of these things it brings everyone down,
> Who cares if injustice is creeping to town?
> Creeping to town.
>
> Drowning souls call out our names,
> We turn and look the other way,
> Don't feel any anger,
> Never be touched by love's mighty flame.
>
> This heart is asleep, locked by fear's chain,
> Don't feel no shame,
> Sleep sleep.

Lights on the CHOIR *fade. The sound of a shop bell as* ELWYN *enters the newsagency.*

ELWYN: No hurry. You're right. Just seeing if the crossword book's come in yet. Serve the others, I'm not in a rush. What letter? My mother'll be writing letters to the editor from her grave. What's it about this time? Come on, tell me. Don't look at me like that, I didn't write the thing. Nothing'd surprise me. They should give her a weekly column. Eighty-six running a shop and on half the committees in town… If you're not going to tell me, I'll buy it.

** © K. Mazzella

Clip it out for Anita. She always likes to know what her Nana's up to next.

ELWYN *picks up the newspaper.*

The *Yarrawonga Chronicle.* My mother's pulpit. A dollar? Is it really? Last time I bought it, it was eighty cents.

ELWYN *steps outside. She and* MAVIS *remain in different parts of the space.*

Lights on MAVIS, *in her chair, as she writes her letters.*

VIDEO: Images of pen to paper. MAVIS*'s letters to the editor. Many of them, fluttering across the screen.*

[*Reading her paper*] You rotten hypocrites. Bloody churches, honestly…

MAVIS: 'Dear Sir. What hypocrisy… these people complaining about young ones playing pinball. What harm can pinball?… John, the owner of the premises… what about adults gambling away on the pokies?…'

ELWYN: [*the paper*] Bloody council, honestly…

MAVIS: 'Dear sir! A humble slice of bread… food for the birds, bread and butter pudding, breadcrumbs so they're ready whenever you want them… we need to return to the earth whatever the earth can take.'

ELWYN: She didn't… Mum! Well, this'll get them talking…

ELWYN *exits.*

MAVIS: 'Dear Sir… Pity it's not Dear Madam, but there you are. I write as a mother of nine loved children, about these people who are so much against abortion… would they look after these unwanted children for so much as two hours?… be more concerned with those who are living… standing in judgement on women who find themselves…'

ELWYN *steps into Mavis's space.*

ELWYN: Mum. I've just seen a notice in our shop window. A political type of thing.

MAVIS: Yes. I put it there.

ELWYN: People 'round here, they've got 'Coalition, National Party' embroidered on their bedheads.

MAVIS: Well, they might like something different to think about.

ELWYN: Joan Stevenson says she'll stop doing business with us.

MAVIS: What did she come in for?

ELWYN: Two metres of lining for the going away outfit.

MAVIS: Did she buy it?

ELWYN: Yes... but it nearly killed her.

MAVIS: As long as she got her wallet open before she dropped. [*Back to her letter writing*] East Timor.

> *The sound of volleys of gunfire.* MARIANA *appears. She stands on top of the central container, her baby on her hip.*

'Dear Sir... As East Timor prepares for the referendum for independence...'

VIDEO: Images of the build-up to the elections in East Timor.

'... signs of violence coming from Indonesian troops and the militias... real protection... proper peace-keeping now before it's too late.'

VIDEO: Images of the militia, driving through the roads and villages of East Timor.

> MARIANA, *uncertain, is interviewed by a journalist (unseen).*

MARIANA: I never give interview before. Something you don't understand you must ask again. Thank you for coming to our country. Now as we get closer to referendum day, we must have the eyes of the world. This country has been slow massacre for twenty-five years, I can say that. When we hear Habibe call for referendum, people of course are dancing in the street. But dancing only on one foot, ready to run to hiding on the other. Please report to your newspapers—

> *She asks a person nearby, in Tetum, if she's doing all right? They tell her yes, so she continues.*

[*Urgent*] I ask am I saying it the way you can understand. These militia killing people everywhere, this is not civil war. Indonesian army, they are giving guns, they are giving orders. Boys they can have motor bikes if they join the militia. I am telling you the truth, okay? Or the militia come bang on the door. Your fifteen-year-old sister, let's have her. So of course he join militia. Their strong message: vote for independence you are dead. Please, journalists. Please ask the UN this. Please don't believe Indonesian police protect papers of ballot on day we vote. It is the police stand back watch the militia do their dirty work. [*In Tetum*] Please can you ask UN, the police are not right for job of the ballot. [*Pause.*] Now I take you to Hera. To see the grave of students. Students from the Polytechnic. Yes.

VIDEO: *Images of people lining up to vote in East Timor, and of hands marking ballots.*

MAVIS: You watched it on television. The people walking miles and miles over mountains lined up at six in the morning to cast their vote after all that intimidation. And there we are complaining there's not enough parking outside the primary school on election day.

VIDEO: *Still image of the final results:*

Attendance—98.5% registered voters
For independence—78.5%
For autonomy—20.5%

Segue into VIDEO: *Images of the post-ballot destruction.*

I couldn't take my eyes off those poor Australian Federal Police, those UN officials locked in with the refugees. Imagining, if you stop to imagine, imagining knowing they were being ordered to turn their back on all those people who relied on them. Knowing that if they're made to abandon that United Nations compound, so many people will die.

TRANSITION

The sounds of gunfire and confusion.

MARIANA: I can't find my baby!

MARIANA has just climbed over the UN compound wall. The noise should be enormous—people calling, crying, etc.

[*In Tetum*] I can't find my baby. Can you please?… Can someone?… Yes, I know I'm not the only one… He's wearing a blue shirt, blue pants… There! There!

A CHOIR *member passes her baby to her.* MARIANA *finds him, holds him tight. The baby's face, unseen by us, has been scratched.*

Okay? Yes, he's okay. Okay… You are nurse? UN nurse? [*She is.*] Just some scratching from… how you call it—razor-wire… Oh, his little face…

The sound of shooting. MARIANA *drops to the ground. The noise of people continues. The shooting stops.*

I was outside compound, come inside just now… I throw him over the wall there. Razor-wire, yes. What kind of women we become, throw our babies over a wall?… Hey… hey… please. Please tell UN give us time—warning—give us warning when they say that's it, they're out of here. Just so we got time to run… [*Another person*] Journalist, you. Yes, I can give interview now. Yes, I can tell you what is happening in Dili if we can find somewhere quiet…

The sound of volleys of gunfire. The noise of people intensifies. MARIANA *is still crouched, protecting her baby.*

[*To the journalist*] I know shooting. That's just shooting in the air. Not shooting to us. Shooting to frighten. They're doing a good job, eh.

She sees signs that the UN is preparing to leave.

Oh look… Oh God… Journalists, UN staff… Oh God, you're giving us your things! Tins of milk, bottles of water, bits of clothes. Because you going to evacuate, aren't you? Aren't you? Tonight, is it? Tonight? All looking down, ashamed. [*Pause.*] What we all must look to you. Like we're all victims waiting for the kill. But this is only now. Until this happen so many people doing something to fight. Everyone. Maybe you think I'm poor helpless mother, victim. No. Until my baby came, I was woman soldier. In Falantil. Guerilla soldier in the mountains. Yes. Actually I was *commandante*. Biggest secret of my life, not even my cousins know. So at least if we get kill, at last I've told my little story. Something I give to you. In exchange for tins of milk.

The noise level has risen during the above. The CHOIR *members (as refugees) start to wail.* MARIANA *is given an order by someone.*

What? Calm them down? [*In Tetum*] Everyone should be quiet, the UN says everyone calm down here!

The noise intensifies.

These people are fear for a reason. When you leave only choice we got is pick up our kids and run up, up, up into those hills. This is not choice.

MARIANA *decides to sing to the panicking crowd. Slowly the noise fades and the* CHOIR *gradually joins…*

SONG: 'No Woman, No Cry' ***

MARIANA:

> *Loron Ida*
> *O Tur Iha Tasi Ibun*
> *O tur Iha Fatuk*
> *Ida Nia leten*
> *Matan Been Suli Hela*
> *Tansa Mak O Tanis*

The CHOIR *joins in at chorus.*

CHOIR:

> *La La Bele Tanis*
> *La La Bele Tanis*
> *La La Bele Tanis*
> *La La Bele Tanis*

MARIANA:

> *Hau Sei Tanis*
> *Tanba O husik Hau*

*** © Rai Abut (Tetum lyrics). Music by Bob Marley.

Hadomi Neba Hau Hota Ona
Laran Dodok Tebes
Susar Loos Bebeik

CHOIR:

La La Bele Tanis
La La Bele Tanis
La La Bele Tanis
La La Bele Tanis

TRANSITION

MAVIS *drafts a very important letter.*

MAVIS: 'Mr Alexander Downer.' [*Correction*] 'The Honourable. Minister for Foreign Affairs.' I won't make that joke but you always think it, don't you? 'Parliament House. Canberra… whether there would be any obstacles to my…'

SONG: 'Happy Birthday'

The CHOIR *begins to sing 'Happy Birthday'.*

VIDEO: Images of a birthday party. Small hands being held by older ones, presents being handed over. Little children passing around food. Precious, simple moments. Everyone should be entitled to such fortune.

Sparklers are lit by the CHOIR *during the above, as the happy birthday song stops abruptly.*

A knife glints in the light. MAVIS *is poised to cut the cake.* ELWYN *is in the corner, with a glass of wine.*

MAVIS: Well, thank you, children, and grandchildren, and great grandchildren, for giving me this lovely party. A really lovely party. I really don't know why you're making such a fuss, it's not that hard to get to eighty-six, all you have to do is keep breathing. Thank you all for your gifts and all the delicious food, we mustn't let any of it go to waste. Now I do have something to say to you all. Something I've been waiting to say until I got you all together. You've all been wondering why the film crew's here, and that's because… well…

I've decided to go to East Timor.

Silence.

[*Waving the knife*] Well. I might just cut the air.

Silence.

VIDEO: *Loud flash of images of soldiers, destruction. A montage of all their fears. End with a still of the birthday cake.*

Silence.

MUSICIAN: [*as a young girl*] Nana, I think you're great! Great! Great!

Silence.

MAVIS: Isn't it interesting how it's your grandchildren hold you in higher esteem than your children? [*To the party*] I've still got to work out the nuts and bolts, but look. [*Pulling out a hand-made book*] Someone's made me a home-made dictionary, everything I'll need to know in the language they speak there, Tetum. So I'll be right. I'd like to give the women up there something to do. Something to do other than grieve.

Silence.

I can teach them to sew and cut out patterns. I know what you're thinking—I've never used a pattern for any of you lot in my life, but that's just me. So the idea being the women can get involved, and make some income, and become self-sufficient. Steve and his crew are going to make a little documentary about it. About my trip. About East Timor. [*Pause.*] Which is, as I said… where I'll be going. Quite soon actually. So you won't have a lot of time to get used to it. [*Pause.*] You've only got to go out on that footpath right now and look at what we all throw out—three-quarters of that stuff the East Timorese could use. And what with the GST coming in… my shop's going to be… All the bits and pieces I sell, I'm likely to drown in paperwork.

ELWYN: Sorry. Where exactly is East Timor? Where exactly are we talking about? [*Defensive*] Well, I don't read newspapers. [*Stressed*] Which is why I don't get stressed.

VIDEO: Flash image of a globe turning to show East Timor in relation to Australia.

VIDEO: Footage of Mavis's children and grandchildren commenting on her announcement, ending with: 'You can help the people from here.'

Doesn't surprise me. Well, it doesn't. Remember Mrs Wheeler? The Wheelers. Poor as church mice. That day one of them came running in. Someone's left all these pyjamas and nighties at our gate and they fit! Brand new ones. For me and all the boys! That was Mum. It was. It was. Look, don't tell me, I know. It was, she told me. You go and ask her. It was her.

> MAVIS *enters.*

MAVIS: What are you squabbling about?

ELWYN: Nothing.

MAVIS: Well. That was nice. That was Anita ringing to say happy birthday from Byron.

ELWYN: Nite? Is she still on the phone?

MAVIS: I told her the news. She thinks it's a great idea. Good on you, Nan, she said. She's already given me some ideas.

ELWYN: There'll be no shortage of ideas. The main one being you're crazy. You've never even been overseas.

MAVIS: Tasmania. Well, you've got to start sometime. You know what she said? 'You and I could travel together, Nan.'

ELWYN: She's always been a good little traveller, Nite. She was great in New Zealand.

MAVIS: She said she thought she might come with me. 'If Mum didn't mind.' If you wouldn't worry. [*Pause.*] Well. It is all very interesting. You lose faith in the younger generation sometimes, then they're the ones who don't have a problem.

ELWYN: I didn't say I had a problem, Mum. [*Pause.*] I don't have a problem.

MAVIS: Good.

ELWYN: I don't.

MAVIS: We thought perhaps you could run the shop while we're there.

This could all work out!

ELWYN *is left alone in the space.*

MUSIC

VIDEO: Images of TV news and other footage of East Timor. Burnt-out buildings. Australian troops. End on an image of a female Falantil soldier. Year 2000.

MARIANA, *in her Falantil uniform, leans forward to be presented with a commemorative tais. She is proud, fighting tears.*

MARIANA: [*in Tetum*] Thank you. I am honoured. Thank you to all my fellow soldiers. And to all those clandestine who support us over the years. *Timór Lorosa'e!*

CHOIR: [*raising fists in a salute*] *Timór Lorosa'e!*

ELWYN *is pouring over a national newspaper, sitting in Mavis's chair.* MAVIS, *quietly pleased, watches her closely.*

MAVIS: I keep waking up thinking… the worst thing you could do, I think, is build up women's hopes and dash them to pieces. That would really be terrible, wouldn't it?

ELWYN: [*reading*] '…estimates that thousands of women and children have been left alone, not knowing when, or if, their husbands and fathers will return.' Thousands.

MAVIS *lightly strokes her daughter's head.*

On another part of the space, a journalist is asking MARIANA *questions.*

MARIANA: Yes, you can have photo. Yes, I am Mariana, yes. Yes, I was Fretilin *commandante*, that's true. Yes, I am one came down from mountains to have my baby, then go back up to fight. [*Pause.*] My aunty, she mind him, yes. [*Pause.*] I answer your question with a story. A story about mothers. In September '99 after we vote when things were in last days I was back at my aunty's place. I give myself job. Take sacks UN rice to refugees here in Dili. Next door my house my neighbour like everyone, many people staying there. Hiding. This one boy, twelve years, he sees me in truck to take rice, can he come? I ask mother, she says yes. [*Swallowing some tears*] Sorry. I just remember I hand my baby to her, say sorry dirty nappy, sorry. [*Pushing herself to tell this story*] So he was in back of truck, this boy. And all of a sudden the window at the back it was red. Aitarak militia, they just cut off his head. Drag body away. I have to tell mother. I don't know how to tell you this, but this has happen. And that mother she say, [*first in Tetum, then she translates it into English*] as she hand my baby back to me... 'Well. I don't blame you. We're all nearly living or dying every day. And this is the day my son died.' I have to be strong like her because my baby boy, he's not here today. My boy he was brave. Lasted two weeks after UN left. My baby was special for me. Not special for my country.

MUSIC

MARIANA *begins marching on the spot.*

SONG: 'Timor Woman'****

ELWYN:

> Timor woman I sing to you cross the wire

CHOIR:

> Timor woman—Hu!

ELWYN:

> Timor woman I sing to you cross the sea

CHOIR:

> Timor woman—Hu!

ELWYN:

> You're a fighter, you fight for your child
> Just like me

CHOIR:

> Timor woman—Hu!
> Timor woman—Hu!

MARIANA:

> Raped, left alone, shackled, yet still she stands

CHOIR:

> Timor woman—Hu!

****   © K. Mazzella

MARIANA:

> *Companiera,* her heart and mind never give in

CHOIR:

> Timor woman—Hu!

MARIANA:

> Hear her song of freedom for every child, woman and man

CHOIR:

> Timor woman—Hu!
> Timor woman—Hu!

ELWYN:

> Lonely, abandoned, abused—yet still I stand

CHOIR:

> Timor woman—Hu!

ELWYN:

> Timor woman, once I lived with a drunk, angry man

CHOIR:

> Timor woman—Hu!

ELWYN:

> You feel so helpless when the kids cry: 'Mum, where's our dad?'

CHOIR:

> Timor woman—Hu!
> Timor Woman—Hu!

ELWYN / MAVIS:

> So many boys and men taken away

CHOIR:

> Timor woman—Hu!

ELWYN / MAVIS:

> Tortured, murdered, taunted, enslaved

CHOIR:

> Timor woman—Hu!

ELWYN / MAVIS:

> Timor's children must live to see better days

CHOIR:

> Timor woman—Hu!

ELWYN / MAVIS:

> *Companiera,* our hymn of freedom guides us to a new day.

CHOIR:

>*Libertade! [Freedom!]*
>*Libertade! [Freedom!]*

ELWYN / MARIANA:

>*Companiera,* I feel what you're going through

MAVIS: [*answering*]

>*Companiera,* I feel what you're going through

CHOIR:

>Timor woman—Hu!

ELWYN / MARIANA:

>Linked by a spirit that moves in us when we give birth

MAVIS: [*answering*]

>Linked by a spirit that moves in us when we give birth

CHOIR:

>Timor woman—Hu!

ELWYN & MAVIS: [*together*]

>We sing for all fighters, all mothers across the world

CHOIR:

>Timor woman—Hu!

ELWYN & MAVIS: [*together*]

>Who do what they must for their children inherit the earth

CHOIR:

>Timor woman—Hu!

ELWYN & MAVIS: [*together*]

>Inherit the earth

CHOIR:

>Timor woman—Hu!

ELWYN & MAVIS: [*together*]

>Inherit the earth

CHOIR:

>Timor woman—Hu!
>Timor woman—Hu!
>Timor woman—Hu!

Container doors open to reveal Mavis's shop. ELWYN *has some scissors and is slicing off lengths of fabric on a table.* MAVIS *enters and starts helping her.*

ELWYN: I've been talking to Anita.

MAVIS: Oh.

ELWYN: Oh what?

MAVIS: Telling her not to go?

ELWYN: Telling her I'm coming too.

MAVIS: You didn't tell me.

ELWYN: I'm telling you now.

MAVIS: As long as you're sure.

ELWYN: I've spent two weeks thinking about it. You'll need someone to show them how to fix the machines. Apart from everything else. We could go up ahead of you and set things up.

MAVIS: You know that time you said you'd always wondered what you'd been put on this earth for…

ELWYN: Don't be so bloody flowery, Mum. I'm coming, that's enough.

MAVIS: It'll be the making of you.

ELWYN: I'm already fully-made.

MAVIS: Get ready for a lot of Rotary and Lions Club dinners. When they make dirty jokes, pretend you don't understand.

TRANSITION

> MAVIS *is giving one of her speeches.*
>
> *On another part of the space, through the following,* MARIANA *sews together some sections of black fabric which will make a loose-fitting mourning dress.*

Thank you for inviting Elwyn and myself to tell you about Timor. Of course we haven't been there yet, but so far that hasn't stopped me talking about it as if I had! Perhaps because I knew a chappie who fought in East Timor in the war, and I can always remember him saying, if it wasn't for the Timorese he would never have come back home. Sixty thousand Timorese people died protecting Australian soldiers, just about twenty times the population of Yarrawonga. Until we landed they were all neutral. Ever since then don't you think we should have been looking out for those people, but of course money's got more weight than friendship sometimes, where countries are concerned anyway. So at least now we can make amends. There's an enormous container down at the *Chronicle*, apparently the people really have lost everything if you can imagine that, I'll give you an idea of what I've been told they need in the first instance, but first of all I'd like to thank the Lions Clubs of Warrandyte, Mildura, Kerang and Echuca for the wonderful Ford Fairlane utility that will be part of the first container load to go. It's terribly urgent that we try to get these women back on their feet. A help up. They're saying so many, many babies have died. From what I glean, as far as children's clothing's concerned, we should concentrate on toddlers aged one year and up.

Very self-consciously, ELWYN *reads from a list.*

ELWYN: 'Sewing machines, of course, treadle and electric, any buttons, cottons, fabric you might have. Exercise books for the kiddies, clothing, utensils, pots and ladles, clothes for adults and children. Shelving, shelving brackets, musical instruments, crockery, toys, bicycles, office equipment. Pens, pencils, whiteboards, blackboards, paper…'

MAVIS: [*fielding questions*] Am I scared? I can't see the point of being scared. No, I tell a lie. I am utterly terrified of those clowns in Yarrawonga in Easter backing out into oncoming traffic as if they were blindfolded. They'd frighten the feathers off a goose. But people, no. People are people everywhere. [*Another question*] No, no, the idea is a co-operative. No, it's not a factory for us to make money, oh no, nothing like that. [*Another question*] Yes, we've linked up with someone very good, recommended by someone else. So our first co-operative will be at Metinaro. On the coast, just over the hills from Dili, behind that hundred-foot high Jesus on the point. This chap, Frank, he's teaching permaculture, he's full of ideas, so Metinaro's where we'll be.

ELWYN: No, not even CARE Australia gets concessions on sending their containers, so Malcolm Fraser tells us, so we will have to pay full price.

Above them, on top of the container, MARIANA *takes off her Falantil uniform and puts on a black dress.*

MAVIS: In conclusion, if you can imagine all those mothers when they had to run to the hills, how those babies died. An adult can live on nuts and berries and bits of grass. Babies need so much more.

SONG: 'Angry Love's Name' *****

ELWYN:

> What do I pack,
> To take away, the sadness
> Inside my heart?
> I've stored secrets
> That won't see
> The light of day.
> Just like secrets buried in a country lane,
> Like sad bones abandoned in a drain.

CHOIR:

> Pack! Pack it up! Pack it away!
> Pack! Pack it up! Pack it away!

Still in the shop, ELWYN *packs things up,* MAVIS *trails a long fax.*

MAVIS: Look at this, a thirty-page fax from Metinaro! Frank's so full of bright ideas. That we set up a cafe next door to the co-op—that's additional income for the women, so we'll need to squeeze some tables and chairs into that container… I was thinking, once we get a few centres going, we could set up mannequin parades, something like that.

ELWYN: Let's wait and see.

MAVIS: I think that really could be something.

ELWYN: And I'm just saying let's wait and see.

MAVIS: We really have to do this properly, don't we? Really follow through. We'll probably have to be a lot more patient up there.

ELWYN: If you're meaning me, just come out and say it.

MAVIS: Both of us.

During the following MAVIS, ELWYN *and* CHOIR *members pack a container with boxes, sewing machines and fabrics.*

The song, 'Angry Love's Name', continues.

MAVIS:

> What did we do in '75?
> We could have helped
> But we turned a blind eye.

***

***** © K. Mazzella

They saved our brothers in the war,
Yet in their hour of need
We ignored them all.
A blood bath, just next door.

ELWYN:

We fought in our kitchens,
Weeping and sore,

ALL:

While you lay bleeding,
I'm so sorry Timor,
I'm so sorry Timor.

CHOIR:

Pack! Pack it up! Pack it away!
Pack! Pack it up! Pack it away!
Pack! Pack it up! Pack it away!
Pack! Pack it up! Pack it away!
Timor Leste Timor Leste x 3

MAVIS:

What secrets lie curled up,
Locked away in dark rooms?

ELWYN:

I hear voices of young men
Cut down in their very bloom.

ALL:

Dirty, guilty, murderous shame,
How can you stifle the awful truth's flame?

MAVIS / ELWYN:

But in the end it returns
To shout out its name,
Its name,
All in angry love's name.

CHOIR:

Pack! Pack it up! Pack it away!
Pack! Pack it up! Pack it away!
Pack! Pack it up! Pack it away!
Pack! Pack it up! Pack it away!
Timor Leste, Timor Leste x 3
Oh, Timor, Timor Timor Leste… Ahhhhh.

As the song ends...

MAVIS: I don't know there's a lot more we can fit in that. You'll keep me posted, won't you? On how you're going.

ELWYN: Actually, Mum, the secret plan's to just take all this loot and shoot through. Me and Nite set up an op shop in Darwin. Fifty brand new sewing machines, I could buy myself a yacht.

MAVIS: I'd like to say it'll be plain sailing.

ELWYN: We'll be right.

> *The last thing to go into the container is a hand-cranked sewing machine.*

MAVIS: Look at this beautiful old hand-crank, not a scratch. It goes like a dream. And it's still got the little transfer on it.

SONG: 'Angry Love's Name' resumes.

ELWYN:
> But it's buried in the heart of our memory,
> Love was betrayed.

MAVIS:
> Lest we forget our history.

ALL:
> How many candles must we light?
> I remember that long dark night.
> In the end it returns
> To shout out its name,
> Its name,
> All in angry love's name.

CHOIR:
> *Timór Lorosae! Timór Lorosae! Timór Lorosae!*

TRANSITION

VIDEO: Sun setting on Dili harbour. Water lapping.

> *Paddling sounds.* ELWYN *is on her mobile.* MAVIS *is in her space.*

MAVIS: Elwyn! Hello! How's it going? How's Anita?

ELWYN: Speaking Tetum already... It kills me.

MAVIS: Where are you?

ELWYN: Cooling off, paddling. Watching the sun set into the sea.

MAVIS: What about the crocodiles?

ELWYN: It's all right, I'm covered in Aeroguard.

MAVIS: If I hear a splash I'll hang up. Wouldn't want to waste the call. How's Metinaro, have you found a building yet?

ELWYN: Not one with a roof. Yet. Which we need to shift that container off the wharf... I tell you, I've got so many kids here, seven or eight years old who literally have no clothes. Nothing.

MAVIS: We've got another container just about full.

ELWYN: Every woman I meet seems to have been left alone. You look around the street and you realise there's this gap.

MAVIS: What gap?

ELWYN: Men between twenty-five and fifty or so. Gone. Everywhere someone's been killed there's these little piles of rocks...

MAVIS: And what's Frank like? Still full of beans? Haven't had a fax for a while. I said, what's Frank like... ?

ELWYN: I'm not big on men who hit their wives.

MAVIS: What are you saying, you're breaking up?

ELWYN: I'm starting to think he just wants what's sitting there in our container. That Frank's come here to set up his white man's kingdom.

MAVIS: [*not hearing*] Well, I'm assuming you can hear me. If I don't manage to call you from Darwin—

ELWYN: Frank, Mum, he's a complete and utter arsehole.

MAVIS: I'll see you at the airport when I land!

ELWYN: Mum, the women, what they really need...

MAVIS: Are you still there, El?... I think you said you need something...

ELWYN: Mum. There are so many women in mourning. They desperately need black fabric. Metres and metres. Rolls and rolls.

MAVIS: Plenty of black fabric... I'll put some in the next container.

TRANSITION

> MARIANA *dances 'The Song of the Black Cloth'.*

SONG: 'The Song of the Black Cloth' ******

****** © K. Mazzella

MUSICIAN: [*solo*]

>Give me black, black cloth
>To wind around a sky that weeps.
>Give me black, black cloth
>To wrap around my raging heart.
>My people's blood flows with the rain,
>The sky is crying, how it stains,
>Mother Earth she knows the pain
>That breaks you open,
>Breaks you open.
>
>Give me black, black cloth
>To wrap around the bride
>Who becomes the widow.
>Give me black, black cloth
>To soak up her bitter tears.
>
>Past the stars, the rain falls down,
>Drifting through the burnt-out towns.
>Windowless the walls resound
>With cries of the dead,
>Cries of the dead.
>
>I want to wear the colour
>That anoints all women's sorrow.
>In the ashes we discover
>We must bury our hearts tomorrow,
>Tomorrow...

INSTRUMENTAL

>Candles burning in the rain,
>The sky is crying, how it stains,
>My dress with sorrow's dark refrain,
>And moans with the wind,
>Moans with the wind.
>
>Give me black, black cloth,
>Give me black, black cloth,
>Give me black, black cloth.

TRANSITION

> ELWYN *appears on top of one of the containers.*

ELWYN: Oi, Frank. Yes, I'm talking to you, Frank, you. I don't see anything getting done here. I see your letters raising funds, you-beaut letters and you get the funds, but I don't see where it's going except on restaurant bills. I see volunteers come for a month, you promise them diplomas and then you piss them off. I see a lot of eating in restaurants, buttering up the UN. I don't see what you're doing for these people. You got us here under false pretences. You've sacked us? You can't sack us, you don't employ us! After all we've promised these women, after all my mother's hard work. My daughter's hard work, my hard work. I want the gear back you've already taken out of that container. Not from the women, it's all for them. But from you. [*Pause.*] Failed in Cape York. Try East Timor. [*To Frank*] Are we what? Are we going back to Australia? No, Great Chief Frank. The thing is you're just a glitch. I've had disappointments in my life, buckets full, and you don't even come close. I'll have sewing centres for these women here if I have to build them with my teeth. [*She moves away. Calling back to Frank*] Yeah, yeah. Make my life hell. We're from Yarrawonga! We know the meaning of work.

> ELWYN *climbs into a taxi. She notices* MARIANA *walking, her arms piled with vegetables.*

Excuse me.

MARIANA: No, not for sale. Taking home. Not for selling.

ELWYN: Would you like a lift? In this taxi? Going to Dili. You?

MARIANA: Dili, yes…

> MARIANA *climbs in. They travel along a little way. The taxi slows.*

It's a roadblock. [*In Tetum*] You must stop.

ELWYN: Portuguese UN. Look at them, as if they own the place. Papers he says. Geez, I hate people who click their fingers. [*Mimicking the soldier*] Get out—now—open boot… Open boot, my arse. [*To* MARIANA] Hold onto your hat, I've had a bad day.

> ELWYN *steps out of the taxi.* MARIANA *watches her fearfully.*

MARIANA: [*in Tetum, to the driver*] Don't worry, keep calm. We've done nothing wrong.

ELWYN: Excuse me, I just heard the way you spoke to this driver. And I didn't hear please, I didn't hear thank you. I did see a gun in the poor boy's face. What's the problem? Oh, now there's no problem, he's driving a *malae*. What, there's suddenly no problem?

MARIANA: *Senhora…*

ELWYN: Now you don't want to look in the boot. But a minute ago you—

MARIANA: *Senhora…*

ELWYN:— you seemed very keen. You want to know what's in the boot. Take a look. That's not a look. Take-a-look. Never mind waving your gun.

MARIANA: [*in Tetum*] Keep your head down.

ELWYN: No one's going anywhere. Never mind your smart blue cap. You apologise to him. Apologise. You're a disgrace to your uniform and a disgrace to yourself. [*Pause.*] Good. You're a guest here now.

She gets back in the car. The sound of the taxi starting up again.

Bugger them. This is your country.

MARIANA *looks back over her shoulder at the soldier.*

MARIANA: [*looking at* ELWYN] You say your mother she's coming tomorrow?

ELWYN: Yes. She is.

MARIANA: Is she like you, your mother?

ELWYN: No, no she's not. Not at all. My mother's a very outspoken sort of woman.

MARIANA *can't imagine what the mother must be like.*

MARIANA: In Australia, were you in army?

ELWYN: The army? No. Why?

MARIANA *shrugs, digesting all this.*

Where did you say you were going?

MARIANA: [*quietly*] Cousin at Vera Cruz.

ELWYN: [*to the driver*] Vera Cruz first, okay?

VIDEO: Images of Vera Cruz.

Oh, my God. What's that? Up on the hill.

MARIANA: Never mind that. Just little bit more to cousin's house…

ELWYN: That big joint. Straight ahead.

MARIANA: Was a hospital. No more.

> MARIANA *speaks in Tetum to the driver about the hospital.*

ELWYN: They rebuild?

MARIANA: Indonesian special hospital. Military.

ELWYN: Many women live up here?

MARIANA: Many yes. [*Showing the vegetables*] My cousins.

ELWYN: I've found it. A building with a roof.

TRANSITION

MUSIC

VIDEO: Images of Mavis's arrival.

> *At the airport,* MAVIS *arrives.* ELWYN *greets her, takes her bag, She introduces her to* MARIANA.

It's a building, but that's all it is. There's miles of red tape to get through before we even think about getting women in. There's about one and a half power points, no electricity, windows and doors all gone—

MAVIS: But a roof. That's a start.

ELWYN: That's Colonel Nemo from Norway. Meeting you for the film crew. You'll probably have to go back on the tarmac and pretend you've just arrived.

> MAVIS *takes her bag and heads back from the plane again as if crossing the tarmac for the first time.*

MAVIS: Yes, it is. My first trip overseas. Yes, I suppose I have chosen an unusual destination, yes… Was it really? All still burning when you arrived?… Oh, dear… Sewing centres for the women. Give them some independence… We'll go whatever way you think is best…

VIDEO: Images of the destroyed Dili.

> MAVIS, *affected by what she's just seen, is outside* MARIANA*'s cousin's house.*

MAVIS: El, I wonder... how long did it take you to?... You seem used to all the... destruction...

ELWYN: Mum, listen. Vera Cruz won't happen straight away. I'm not sure Frank didn't fire off some letters. To where it hurts. Nothing for you to worry about, that's what I'm here for.

MAVIS: What I'm thinking is it's better if I'm staying somewhere where I'm paying rent to someone who... where I could be of assistance...

VIDEO: Mariana's cousin's house in Dili.

MARIANA: You have coffee here. My cousin house.

MAVIS: If we can just get that next container off the wharf.

ELWYN: Once we're in Vera Cruz.

MARIANA: You stay here—my cousin's house.

ELWYN: You're not staying here.

MARIANA: I make coffee for the film crew.

> MAVIS, *in a chair, is being interviewed.*

MAVIS: I knew it would look pretty battered, but it was really depressing to see so much destruction. It just really has been terrible. Perhaps I didn't need that drive around on my first day. But you see all the destruction of the beautiful buildings that are sort of left... all the fittings just gone. And you wonder, don't you? How the people who did the looting—never mind what side they were on—how they could feel good about... about using the things they've taken. You'd think it'd prey on your mind. [*She leans down to rub her legs.*] Sorry, the plane blew my legs up. The Colonel was telling me about the targeting of teachers and skilled people... taken out to sea in barges and just shot. You can't imagine. But still. You see the people smile. They're looking forward to something better and that's just how we've all gotta be.

> ELWYN *enters from inside the house.*

ELWYN: My mother can't use that toilet.

MAVIS: [*to* ELWYN] Colonel Nemo said they looted the showers and toilets, took them to West Timor.

ELWYN: Mum.

MAVIS: They could use the money. The toilet doesn't bear thinking about, but there we are.

MARIANA: If you stay here Australian agency, someone, they can ask please get new toilet.

MAVIS: Now you're talking, Mariana. That's what we call leverage. You tell whoever you need to, I'm staying here. And I'm an old lady. When I go to the toilet I need to sit down.

> ELWYN *leaves.* MAVIS *is distracted.*

MARIANA: What?

MAVIS: The lady walking along... that's just... it's the first baby I've seen since I arrived. And a tiny scrawny thing it is too. [*To* MARIANA] Do you have a family? Children?

> *Pause.*

MARIANA: *Avó Mavis.* Maybe now... that question. Womens here... better for now you don't ask.

MAVIS: I wonder, Mariana... I'll need someone to translate.

MARIANA: I don't speak very much English.

MAVIS: I can't pay you very much money.

> MARIANA *lets herself smile at the word play.*

MARIANA: Not for money. For the womens at Vera Cruz.

TRANSITION

> *Vera Cruz. The three women are some hours into another frustrating meeting.*

ELWYN: Mariana, what's the UN guy saying?

MARIANA: Same as he said before.

ELWYN: What's the chief saying?

MARIANA: Same as yesterday.

MAVIS: About the windows?

MARIANA: About the windows.

ELWYN: Again.

MAVIS: These meetings take longer than the plane trip. I never thought my legs'd blow up from a meeting. Weeks and weeks of meetings. Trying to get the UN to do something.

MAVIS: Now it's about...

MARIANA: Still they are talking about the doors.

ELWYN: About the doors and the window and it's not safe. [*Enough*] I want this building done and what I want to know is who's going to do it for us the best and quickest way. Two and a half months I've been waiting. Waiting for this. Waiting for that—the Timorese people are sick of waiting. Let's forget the UN, let's forget Oxfam. Let's just do it. If we can get some building material—I know it's hard—and at least have some windows and doors, we can start teaching the women and they can start making money. The local people do it for themselves and the money comes later. Hopefully.

MAVIS: They don't have the timber, Elwyn—

ELWYN: I know that.

MARIANA: But something else. Something else no one is telling you.

ELWYN: Frank and his UN letters. I'm in the process of sorting that out.

MARIANA: No. Not that.

ELWYN: What?

MARIANA: Even doors and windows, it's not safe.

ELWYN: We only need to lock the place, it doesn't have to be Fort Knox. Can you take Mum back into town?

TRANSITION

> *Inside another container. Mavis's temporary bedroom. A mosquito net and a campbed.*

MAVIS: Not to be able to start. To just open the container and start... I just feel as if I'm not accomplishing anything, that's the worst of it. That the effort has been wasted because I'm not... well, perhaps I'm not up to what I thought I was up to. I feel more inadequate perhaps than I've felt in a long time. Well. Perhaps I'm just a bit flattened at the moment. Two and a half months, perhaps that just seems long to us. And now my granddaughter's going home. So there'll just be the two of us.

MARIANA: You like me to take the pig outside.

MAVIS: No, no. Well, yes.

> *Pig noises as she chases it outside.*

MARIANA: You feel sad, *Avó Mavis*.

> MARIANA *pulls the mosquito net over* MAVIS.

MAVIS: Sometimes if you just have a lie down… you wake up, things seem different. Anyway, that's what I find. What's the Tetum for sleep?

MARIANA: *Doba.*

MAVIS: And dreams? You know. Pictures when you sleep.

Pause. MARIANA *can't think about dreams.*

MARIANA: You rest, *Avó Mavis.* And please, you don't give up on us.

TRANSITION

Vera Cruz. Dusk. ELWYN *is looking out over Dili.* MARIANA *arrives.*

You should think about other place. Not here.

ELWYN: I've promised the women in the village, they're all ready to start.

MARIANA: They say that, but they're frightened.

ELWYN: What. Of me? Of sewing? Of making some money for themselves, what?

MARIANA: Militia maybe.

ELWYN: They're at the borders.

MARIANA: This place, okay. This hospital. It's last place you come. Really last place. [*Pause.*] Indonesian military hospital. You get torture by police, you get shot by military, you gonna come here let them take out bullet? Saw off your leg, no anaesthetic? That room back there, that's where you get dump if they think you're clandestine. If they think you support Falantil.

ELWYN: But now we're changing it into something else.

MARIANA: No—not just that. The spirits. Bad spirits here. Everyone thinks so. That's why… the men think even they make doors and windows, women they will not be safe.

ELWYN *heads off. She returns with a tent, sleeping mat and lamp. She starts setting up the tent.*

You can't stay here!

ELWYN: Look, even if there are spirits, they'd be the spirits of their families. Why'd they come back to hurt them? If I can sleep here, then they'll know they can sew here. If I'm dead in the morning I'm wrong—you're right.

ELWYN *climbs into the tent.*

VIDEO: Vera Cruz. ELWYN *'s tent with gas lamp burning.*

SONG: 'Mate Mohu' *******

MUSICIAN:
>   *Hau Fan Hau Nia Isin*
>   *Sosa Liberdade*
>   *Hau Ran Fakar Suling Tan Buka*
>   *Dalan Los Hau*
>   *Hau Mate Ka Moris Folin*
>   *Ukun Rasik An*

CHOIR:
>   *Mate Mohu*
>   *Soe Isin Lemorai*
>   *Ruin Naklekar*
>   *Tan Ha Rai Doben*

>   *Mate Mohu*
>   *Soe Isin Lemorai*
>   *Ruin Naklekar*
>   *Tan Ha Rai Doben*

MARIANA: [*in Tetum, spoken*] *Ohla Ohla Lulik*
MUSICIAN: [*translating*] Greetings dear spirits
MARIANA: *Sentidus Pezames*
MUSICIAN: I am sorry for your loss
MARIANA: *Peco Disculpa*
MUSICIAN: I am sorry
MARIANA: *Hau Fuan Moras*
MUSICIAN: I have a sore heart
MARIANA: *Ami La Sala*
MUSICIAN: But I am innocent
MARIANA: *Posso Tur Ho O*
MUSICIAN: Can I sit with you?
MARIANA: *Labele Laran Tuku Tuku*

******* © Anito Matos. See Appendix on pages 44–45 for translation of lyrics.

MUSICIAN: Don't be worried about her. She is our sister, she is our friend.

ELWYN: I keep doing this, they'll see I'm fair dinkum. And I'll sleep here tomorrow night. I'll keep sleeping there until we get windows and doors. Until everyone sees it's safe.

TRANSITION

INSTRUMENTAL: 'Morning In Dili' ********

Celebration breaks out as the containers arrive on trucks.

VIDEO: Image of the two containers coming up the hill to Vera Cruz.

ELWYN: We're on!

MARIANA: *E Hené! E Hené!*

ELWYN: I don't know that all the men are keen on their women working, that might have been half the problem, but…

VIDEO: MAVIS*'s hands undoing the lock on the container. Goods spilling out. Kids on tricycles, men with guitars.* WOMEN *unpacking sewing machines.*

MARIANA: My cousin telling her husband, I would rather die than stay home not go there to learn, we got independence now, that includes women you know!

MAVIS: Come and carry something out!

The CHOIR *and the* WOMEN *unpack as they sing.*

SONG: 'Ho Le Le' (traditional)

CHOIR:

> *Ho Le Le Le*
> *Ho Le Le La*
> *Ho Le Le*
> *La Loi Kana [Chief, please grant us your permission]*
> *Masi Olarinda [To celebrate!]*

ELWYN: This is our security. The husbands bringing this stuff in aren't going to let anything happen to it! Or us!

******** © K. Mazzella

VIDEO: Images of the workshop at Vera Cruz.

MAVIS: First try sewing a straight line—oh well, you've got it... Are you sure she's never sewn before?... [*Another*] Yes, that's good, very good. Oh, it's marvellous. Marvellous... [*To* MARIANA] What are they saying? Oh, it doesn't matter, I get the gist. [*To another*] These are the cards that programme the machines... Well, yes, if you'd like to add a fancy stitch... here... Oh, that's a good way to do it, show me how you did that... Now we should get all the cottons straightened out. Put the colours together then you'll know what to order from Australia... [*To* MARIANA] Why are they laughing?

MARIANA: You an old lady, slow down. Slow down.

MAVIS *laughs and waves them aside.* MAVIS *rushes out.*

[*After her*] And you an old lady doesn't need glasses.

MAVIS *comes rushing back with fabric.*

MAVIS: I can still see an order when it walks in the door. Right! We've got our first order for eighteen mattresses, eighteen cushions and... eighteen something else. For one of the NGOs. [*Explaining*] Non-Government Organisations. El, can you find where that mattress stuffing... I know we packed it in somewhere.

MAVIS *tries to explain using her limited, but graphic Marcel Marceau skills.*

Mattress... covers. For one of the Non-Government Organisations... Human Rights something. So nice bright fabrics. They want them finished by Sunday so... we'll just have to get cracking. And let's try, ladies, in all this chaos, to see if we can get stuff to match for the pillowslips.

As MARIANA, ELWYN *and* MAVIS *struggle with the mattress covers, the two* MUSICIANS *sing...*

SONG: 'Mattresses!' '********

MUSICIANS:
> Mattresses!
> They took the windows and the doors,

******** © K. Mazzella

Mattresses!
They took them all,
But we'll make some more,
Mattresses for you and me,
Finally we can get some sleep.

Don't forget to make the sides wide,
As you cut the cloth
With sharp scissors
Make it deep and soft,
Mattresses for you and me,
Finally I get to earn my keep.

Oh, darling!
Oh, come and see what I brought home.
Darling,
Let's try it out, it's been so long.
Mattresses for you and me,
Finally we can get some peace.

Meanwhile ELWYN *struggles with her teaching bookwork.*

ELWYN: [*spoken*] Your costings here and your… You see if you charge
that… that's not enough… Let's say this dress you've just made…
how much lace… how much fabric… your time. You see? So if you
value your time and let's say so much rupiah… Of course at the
moment the fabric, the lace, that's not costing you anything, to get
you on your feet… How can I explain?

The song, 'Mattresses!', resumes.

MUSICIANS:
We're going to sell them
To the NGOs.
Oh, what a bargain,
Sold for a song I know.
A little money for the family,
A little business for my sisters and me,
Finally we'll get back on our feet.

The song ends.

ELWYN *is swamped with paperwork.*

MARIANA: She doesn't want to charge for making this dress.

ELWYN: Sorry?

MARIANA: This is for her family. She doesn't want to charge.

ELWYN: Okay, that's up to her.

MARIANA: She's upset because you make her charge her family.

ELWYN: Not at all, I was saying that *if* she was charging—

MAVIS: I'm going to have a class. How to make bags. To carry their things in.

ELWYN: I can teach bags. What I can't do is all this lingo. The stuff Frank could bullshit through. Application to become an NGO, application to become a charity…

MAVIS: [*to the* WOMEN] Just take whatever pieces you fancy.

ELWYN *watches her mother's lesson.*

Now you see… you make two bags. One's the lining, one's the outside. Making the corners nice and sharp… turn the edge in, top stitch and turn the handle in as you go. The bag's complete. Yes, I think that's all clear, anyway have a go. And if you want to put in a little purse, just sew on a square.

ELWYN: Why don't you show them how to make a zip purse? Attach it to the handles, then they can just flip it in and out.

MAVIS: No, I think we'll just stick to the plain purse.

ELWYN: Your money falls out with just a pocket like that.

MAVIS: A plain purse for now.

ELWYN: A zip purse is more secure.

MAVIS: It's harder to sew.

ELWYN: But people couldn't steal their money.

MAVIS: But we're not doing zip purses today.

ELWYN: Oh well, okay, you run the place.

MAVIS: Well, that was the general idea.

A woman passes ELWYN *with a tray.*

MARIANA: For *Avó*. For Mavis.

MAVIS *sits, someone massaging her legs and feet.*

ELWYN: Yes, I know what *Avó* means. *Avó*, eat this. *Avó*, I do your feet today.

MARIANA: Timorese people respect elder.

ELWYN: Yes, good on them. Frankly I wouldn't mind something delicious to eat. Given all the fucking work… If that fucking Ford Fairlane ute breaks down one more fucking time—every time it doesn't start everything I've spent hours packing has to come out because you can't leave anything anywhere because everything disappears in a breath because everyone's so bloody needy… Sorry. I came here to help. To be nice. Not cranky.

MAVIS: [*calling across the space*] Well, you haven't succeeded.

ELWYN: I'll always be fourteen to you. I can't win.

MAVIS: You'll always be cranky—I don't know about fourteen.

TRANSITION

> *The* WOMEN *exit. Another day.* MARIANA *finds* ELWYN, *standing, looking out over the space.*

ELWYN: Where's Francesca and Aliana and all those ladies? We haven't seen them for days. You don't think they're going to stop coming, do you?

MARIANA: [*lying*] I don't know.

ELWYN: And now Ida and Rosa aren't here… [*To some* WOMEN] You can all keep going, remember yesterday I showed you… You don't have to wait for me to be here watching. Just go for it. If you make a mistake then… it doesn't matter if you make a mistake. No one's going to rouse.

> ELWYN *sits, then* MARIANA, *their legs dangling over the edge of the container.*

[*To* MARIANA] If I taught you, would you like to learn to do the books? For Vera Cruz? I can teach you.

MARIANA: I never do financial before.

ELWYN: I know that. Would you like to learn?

MARIANA: I left school age thirteen. Could not go back.

ELWYN: Like me.

MARIANA: No, I don't think so.

ELWYN: I got out of school the second I could. I asked Mum what time was I born… So on my birthday at twelve-thirty, and the teacher was at the blackboard, I put my hand up and said thanks very much I'm out of here.

MARIANA *is quiet, weighing up whether or not to say...*

MARIANA: I couldn't go back to school because at Dili massacre, in Santa Cruz cemetery, 1991, I got a bullet in my leg. Three days in friend's house we try to squeeze it out. All the time the army come looking for me. Sorry, Tia Elwyn, not the same as you.

Pause.

ELWYN: But you know why, don't you? Why the women come one day, then not come the next? Even though they seem to enjoy it so much. [*Pause.*] I saw those students with my own eyes, coming up the path to learn to sew, and someone—Rosa?—shooing them away.

MARIANA: I'm not sure for the training to learn accounts. I think about it okay?

TRANSITION

MAVIS *enters, packed ready to go home.* ELWYN *enters, slamming down a box. She is oblivious to* MAVIS*'s sadness.*

ELWYN: I lost my temper. I took those boxes of clothes up to the hills. I've been saying for weeks you've got to share this stuff, get it up where it's still really needed. Everyone's hoarding.

MAVIS: I suppose they think if it happens again...

ELWYN: So I just stopped four times between here and Dare. Left it there on the side of the road, for someone. They're all out there staring at the empty ute. You didn't! Yes, I did. And I'll do another trip and another until we distribute more fairly. Well, there we are, my twenty-eighth emotion for the day...

MAVIS: The shop's in a muddle. At home. Apparently it's pretty ghastly. I have to go back.

Only now does ELWYN *stop. She takes in* MAVIS *and her suitcase.*

ELWYN: Change that to twenty-nine.

MAVIS: Apparently it's all pretty ghastly. People like a happy shop and it all sounds a mess. The bank wants me back to fix things up.

They walk slowly, MAVIS *wheeling her bag behind her.*

SONG: 'Angry Love's Name' (one line)

MUSICIAN:

I'm so sorry, Timor…

ELWYN *and* MAVIS *hug goodbye.*

ELWYN: I've been pretty crabby. Sorry.

MAVIS: Oh, well. As long as you noticed, I suppose.

MUSIC

> *Time has passed.* MAVIS *is in Australia,* ELWYN *in Dili. They talk on the phone.*

MAVIS: You must be running out of fabric.

ELWYN: It's all a bit… slow… I can't seem to get them to stick at it.

MAVIS: I'd have the other container on the way but people don't know how to pack. I said to this volunteer—

ELWYN: I went to a village who said they were keen to set up another centre, but there's so much politics, the trouble is they're all so scared of someone else getting more, they're losing chances everywhere.

MAVIS: You're breaking up a bit. Then I said to this volunteer, pack clothes well into the container and jam them up against other things, they should come out without a wrinkle on them. She said, what does it matter, they're getting them for nothing. So I've let her go. If you can let a volunteer go… [*Pause.*] Anyway I've packed you a treadle someone gave in mint condition, and some more tailor shears. [*Pause.*] What are they sewing at the moment?

> MAVIS *packs some fabric into a container.* ELWYN, *in Timor, takes bolts of fabric out as if unpacking. Time passes.*

ELWYN: Some days we're down to just four women.

MAVIS: Oh.

ELWYN: Some of them have had funerals, of course…

MAVIS: And funerals take two weeks…

ELWYN: But even so, the others are only turning up in fits and starts. I don't seem to be able to… to motivate them or something.

MAVIS: You're sleeping better though?…

ELWYN: And the fights to get that other container off the wharf… I'm… I… I need a break. I think. Yeah, I do. I do. Just to…

MAVIS: Well, the last thing those women need is someone who's a bundle of nerves. You take a break.

Lights on MAVIS *fade.*

ELWYN: [*to* MARIANA] Tell the ladies this is my ticket here... Here are the dates I leave, and when I come back. You can see here, Bangkok return. Return. I'm not leaving. Only for a short time. I'm coming back. [*In Tetum*] *Hau Sai Fila Fali.* [*I come here again.*]

MARIANA *translates.* ELWYN *farewells the* WOMEN.

MAVIS, *at home, is visited by her doctor.*

MAVIS: Thank you, doctor, I think I'll be right. Just something I picked up... Yes, that's right. All this stuff here in the bedroom, in the living room, all to the back verandah, it's all going to East Timor. Once I sort it out. Sorting out so that it's all labelled, it's a full-time job. [*Pause.*] I don't know about resting. We're almost ready to send up another container. Resting's not going to get all these things on the ship. And up there where they're needed.

VIDEO: Images of items of clothing, papers being looted.

ELWYN *enters, back from her trip.*

ELWYN: Who did this? All my stuff, all this—plundered. The fucking container! How'd they break the lock!?

MARIANA: You came back.

ELWYN: I said—I said I'm coming back—

MARIANA: They don't know this—

ELWYN: I told them! I—

MARIANA: Yes, but—

ELWYN: The ticket with the return date! Look, I said, I'm coming back, I told you, I told them all. All my things, Christ knows it wasn't much but... Bloody hell. I must be bloody mad to care about anyone here, they sure as hell don't care about me.

MARIANA: They think—

ELWYN: All they had to do was come in and sew. They don't want me here, that's plain as day.

MARIANA: They thought you pissed off home!

ELWYN: I gave my word.

MARIANA: Same as UN. When UN ran away. I can't explain, people don't know who to believe—

ELWYN: Well, they don't trust me. Message received loud and clear.

MARIANA: You're in a country where not even two thousand people can hide safe in a church. Tear gas and shot when they step outside—a church not even safe.

ELWYN: I know.

MARIANA: Betray and trust. They grow like vines together. The same.

ELWYN: No, they're not...

MARIANA: Here they are. When we run from UN compound, right, we're all slipping on stones, all so dark. Trying to carry my baby... This man he was giving us a hand. Like he is leading us to safety. He was not. He was trying to take us to TNI soldiers waiting with their guns. My story is not he was bad man. My story is when he held my arm, when his fingers pressed into my skin, it felt same. Same as someone who is helping you. Same pressure on your arm as someone you really should trust.

ELWYN: Tell me what I should do. To make this a place, where women feel safe together. Where they want to come.

MARIANA: The job was done before you came to Dili.

ELWYN: What job, Mariana?

MARIANA: Doesn't matter

ELWYN: I don't understand.

> *Pause.*

MARIANA: You see that house there. Over there. Many years ago, military told people womens there were prostitutes. Because they think they are clandestine. Still some people believe that. That's Ida and her aunty. So when you start up centre. Some people still believe they are. Why does she stop coming to centre? Ida, they say, we don't sew with her.

MUSIC: 'No Woman, No Cry' (Bob Marley) underscores the following.

Rosa and Francesca, you wonder when they don't turn up. Nine months they go to prison, when they are seventeen. Raped many times. Rosa get the electric. Here. They get the drug in arm so can't have babies. But never mind get bashed. They don't tell they work clandestine. They never tell. But when they come back, some people don't believe. Think they give names. Names of people who give food to Falantil. So when they think even you now piss off, why shouldn't they take some stuff, get something for themselves. [*Pause.*] Next thing—that lady there you never see, her son disappear in '91 and she never see him again. Secret police tell her, someone in your village they betray your son. But they never say who. How long until she trust again? [*Pause.*] And another girl. You can't see her house from here. She was fourteen. She got burnt with cigarettes and got passed man to man rape by one. Then one other. Timorese interpreter allowed to rape the first because she was prize, a virgin. Then they stamp on her, throw in her a room, beating her very hard on the buttocks, everywhere. All the time they saying, now you have opportunities because of Indonesia. Before you couldn't go to school, before you had poor roads we give you good roads. That girl she started to laugh. And when she laughed they beat her again.********

> The MUSICIAN *sings the first verse of 'No Woman, No Cry'.* MARIANA *laughs through the song.*

> SONG: *'No Woman, No Cry'*********

MARIANA: [*over the music*] If you want to kill me please, but I will not work as a spy. I will not sell my people to you.
ELWYN: [*over the music*] Then she decided to go to the hills and fight with the guerillas. And that girl was you.

> MARIANA *nods yes and allows herself to be embraced by* ELWYN. *Finally she gives in to the pain.*

> The MUSICIAN *continues the song with the* CHOIR *joining in with the final chorus.*

SONG: *'No Woman, No Cry' concludes...*

> *Pause.* MARIANA *quiet in* ELWYN's *arms.*

ELWYN: Oh, look down there, Mariana. The old fella sitting on my one folding chair. I liked that chair.
MARIANA: So does he, now. Recycling.

******** From 'All the time they saying...' to end of speech: inspired by the story of Olga Marail (Sintadewe) in Buibere © Sally-Anne Watson
******** © Bob Marley

ELWYN: And he's wearing my cap.

MARIANA: I would like to learn to do accounts for the centre. If the job's still on.

ELWYN: But if the women can't work in a group that's big enough to make it worthwhile… You don't think they can, do you?

MARIANA: Maybe we can find other way.

TRANSITION

> MAVIS *and* ELWYN *are on the phone to each other.* ELWYN *is in someone's house.*

MAVIS: Everything there still in slow motion?

ELWYN: I took two ute-loads to the orphanage today.

MAVIS: Did they like the guitars?

ELWYN: You know what they said?

MAVIS: Go on. It's a nice clear line.

ELWYN: We have nothing to give you so we'll sing for you. And pray for *Avó Mavis*.

MAVIS: Well, you're past saving, of course.

ELWYN: But today I'm making a swap.

MAVIS: A swap?

ELWYN: Someone with an electric machine here, he used to be a tailor. But now he's in a hut without any power. I need an electric for a lady who wants to sew at home so… he's giving me the electric in exchange.

MAVIS: That's a first. A trade.

> MARIANA *speaks to him in Tetum, translates his thanks. She's laughing.*

ELWYN: He's running round and round it like a puppy—

MARIANA: He says the pair of shears is like Christmas.

MAVIS: I wish I was there to see it. I'd like to see that treadle working.

ELWYN: Me too. Wish you were here.

MARIANA: He says, Greetings Yarrawonga.

MAVIS: Greetings!

ELWYN: They're getting out the music at Vera Cruz tonight. I'll call you so you can hear.

The party at Vera Cruz. Night. ELWYN *steps into the party. She holds the phone up for* MAVIS *to hear.*

SONG: 'Yarrawonga' (traditional)

CHOIR:

> *Hau fila ba ona* Yarrawonga, [*I'm going back to Yarrawonga*]
> *A* Yarrawonga, linger longer,
> *Hau fila ba ona* Yarrawonga,
> Where the skies are always blue.
>
> *Hau fila ba ona* Yarrawonga,
> *A* Yarrawonga, linger longer,
> *Hau fila ba ona* Yarrawonga,
> To the land of the kangaroo.

MAVIS: I won't listen too long.

ELWYN: I haven't done it, Mum.

MAVIS: What's that?

ELWYN: Got even close to it being self-sufficient. Remember how we said if we can get to where we're paying for the cost of the containers?... I'm not even close to that.

MAVIS: You know what I remember most from up there? How the women, when they work in a group, how they hone in on each other. If one's been hit at home, or they're weepy. They'll get help with their sewing, or an extra cup of coffee. How quickly they read each other. They need this. To get out of their houses. Even just for that.

> MARIANA *enters, looking sombre.*

ELWYN: [*to* MAVIS] Something's happened. I better go.

> *They hang up.*

MARIANA: John the chief, he's saying from next month, this centre has to go. He gives the building for something else. [*Pause.*] So now you will go home.

MUSIC: 'No Woman, No Cry' (reprise)

TRANSITION

> ELWYN *is talking to* MAVIS *across the space, as if on the phone.*

MAVIS: This new doctor's made me promise to put a sign on the gate. No donations between two and four. I'm meant to have a nap. At least it'll give me some time to myself to get a bit more sorting done.

ELWYN: We've lost Vera Cruz.

Silence.

And someone's offered me a job here.

MAVIS: Will you take it? This other job?

ELWYN: No.

MAVIS: So I should send you a ticket home.

ELWYN: I'll put Mariana on.

MARIANA: *Bondia, Avó Mavis.*

MAVIS: *Bondia,* Mariana!

MARIANA: This is what we think. Never mind a big centre. Never mind that for now. Make small ones, little group of womens who are family or friend. Just small, maybe three machines. Tia El and I think this is good idea and the women pay for fabric, even just a few rupiah. That way they feel better.

MAVIS: So you don't want a ticket home?

ELWYN: We've already got some of the women from up here linked up with friends in town. Ready to start when we find a place.

MARIANA: More building with roofs now—you'd get a surprise.

ELWYN: As long as you're not thinking of retiring.

MAVIS: I'm only eighty-six, I wouldn't know what to do with myself.

MARIANA: Tomorrow, Mavis, is the anniversary. Two years since the referendum.

MAVIS: I'll light a candle for you. Out in the backyard. Tomorrow night.

ELWYN: Oh, and Mum…

MAVIS: Yes… I can hear you except you're cutting in and out.

ELWYN: Four of the ladies up here are pregnant. And at least two we know of down in town.

MAVIS: Are you saying send up baby clothes?…

ELWYN: Send up baby clothes. Yes…

TRANSITION

MAVIS *is at home, with a small box.*

MAVIS: [*to the audience*] I meant to tell Elwyn about this when she called. When I was sixteen I bought my first sewing machine on time payment. And this is the first thing I made with that machine.

MAVIS *takes off the lid of the box to reveal a fragile piece of fabric, almost in pieces.*

VIDEO: *Image of fabric. An old handkerchief. Layers of sheer fabric.*

'To Mother With Love' I embroidered. All the cross-stitch. Everything. Hours and hours of work I put into this. And even though it's frayed and just about in bits and pieces, the same feeling's there, sort of embedded in the fabric, the same feeling that I sewed in it all those years ago.

She closes the box.

MUSIC *begins.*

MAVIS, *in Yarrawonga, lights a candle under the night sky.*

MARIANA *and* ELWYN *also light candles at little makeshift shrines. The* WOMEN *and the* CHOIR *are bathed in candlelight.*

SONG: *'Ho Le Le Le' [traditional]*

CHOIR:
> *Ho Le Le Le*
> *Ho Le Le La*
> *Ho Le Le*
> *La Loi Kana [Chief, please grant us your permission]*
> *Masi Olarinda* x 4 *[To celebrate!]*

THE END

APPENDIX

p.1 Song translation

SONG: 'Dear Mother' (traditional)

CHOIR: When we are born
we name our land 'Dear Mother'.
Dear mother,
the suffering
is overwhelming.

When we die the earth
shall cover our ears, dear mother.
Dear mother,
the suffering
is overwhelming.

CHORUS
Dear mother,
the suffering
is overwhelming.

When we reach out and can't touch
tears will come to our eyes, dear mother.
Dear mother,
the suffering
is overwhelming.

CHORUS
Dear mother,
the suffering
is overwhelming.

p.29 Song translation

SONG: 'Mate Mohu'

MUSICIAN: I sold my body
to get freedom
My blood has run in every direction

to find the right way
Alive or dead
we will rule ourselves.

CHOIR: Everyone's died
Our bones are scattered
in every direction
because of our lovely country.

Everyone's died
Our bones are scattered
in every direction
because of our lovely country.